To: _____

From: _____

Date: _____

Ciana Publishers is dedicated to changing lives through books. Children will be empowered through the "What Would Jesus Do Series". Through these books, we spread the Good News of Jesus Christ, the hope of glory.

SJvR & LS

Copyright © 2022 by Sybrand JvR & Lucia S.
All rights reserved. Published by Ciana Publishers

This Book is Copyright Protected:
his is only for personal use. You cannot amend, distribute, sell, use, quote, or paraphrase any part of the content within this book without the consent of the author. The Author guarantees all contents are original and do not infringe upon the legal rights of any other person or work.

No part of this book may be reproduced, duplicated, or transmitted in any form by means such as printing, scanning, photocopying, or otherwise, without direct written permission from the author or publisher, except for the use of quotations in a book review and as permitted by the U.S. copyright law.
For permission, contact info@cianapublishers.com.

Disclaimer and Terms of Use:
This book is provided solely for entertainment, motivational and informational purposes.

All Scripture quotations, unless otherwise indicated, are taken from the Holy Bible, New International Version®, NIV®. Copyright ©1973, 1978, 1984, 2011 by Biblica, Inc.TM Used by permission of Zondervan. All rights reserved worldwide. www.zondervan.comThe "NIV" and "New International Version" are trademarks registered in the United States Patent and Trademark Office by Biblica, Inc.TM

Authors – Sybrand JvR & Lucia S

3rd Edition 2024

www.cianapublishers.com

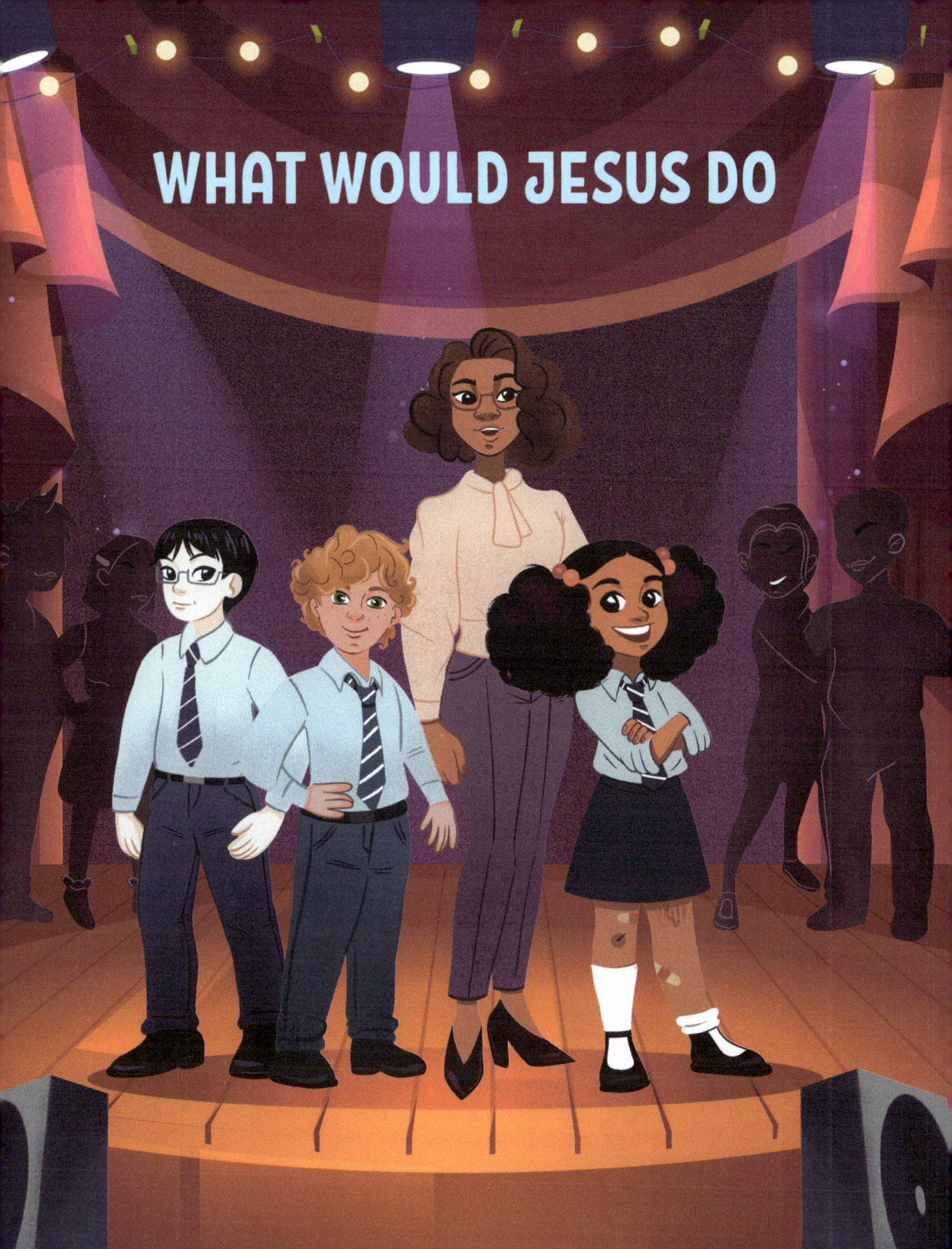

CHARACTER DESCRIPTIONS

Ji-hoon

Ji-hoon mostly dwells in his own world,
being a perfectionist and introverted genius
who is exceptionally loyal. He loves playing chess,
and his dream is to become a great mathematician.
He is well-read and speaks with wisdom. He is calm, calculated,
and very protective and acts like Elsa's big brother.
He loves Jesus a lot and this love overflows to others.

Elsa

Elsa is a bubbly, self-assured go-getter who isn't afraid to speak
her mind and she is quick to act. Her strengths are that she is bold,
confident, and fearless. She loves to dance, play drums,
and play sports. She is always looking for adventure.
As a spontaneous ball of happiness, when she's around,
excitement is sure to follow. Her favourite Bible character is
Esther, who made a big difference in her surroundings.

Ed

Ed is cheerful and friendly and always makes everyone feel welcome.
He adores animals and has two Labrador Retrievers.
Even though he has a dry sense of humour, he likes to laugh
and can make others laugh simply by being himself.
Ed is fun and talkative, and his friends enjoy being around him.

Mrs Wilson

Mrs Wilson loves her students, and they adore her. She is understanding, calm, wise, and firm. She is focused on bringing the best out of her students. She has an exciting way of teaching, using many props and activities in her class. Her constant smile and kindness ensure that students always have a good time.

Bullies

The Bullies are four close friends who are always moving together. To have fun, they mock, and target children they believe are weak. They are rude, enjoy the attention, and try to gain respect by creating fear in kids. They feel superior when they insult children and call them names.

HAVE YOU EVER... DID YOU EVER...

Have you ever been bullied?

Did you ever bully someone?

Do you know of someone who is being bullied?

Have you ever helped someone who has been bullied?

Do you think that Jesus looks out for those who are being bullied?

Little did Ji-hoon and Elsa know that they would come up against a gang of bullies at school.

Wanna see how Ji-hoon and Elsa responded to Ed being bullied?

Let's dive in and find out!

 RUN! Go Ji-hoon! Go faster, Ji-hoon! Big "G" little "o" Go, Go, Go Ji-hoon! No one will catch him now.

 Look at Ed, falling over his own feet.

 Ed, you're not fast; you're last. You fail like a snail and look pale. HAHAHA!

 Hey! At least Ed is trying. STOP being mean. You don't even try!

 We have better things to do.
Ed should stop trying. He is making a fool of himself.
Just look at him! HAHAHA!

 Is giving insults the best you can do?
BACK OFF!

 Guys have some water.

 Ed?... Never! You barely ran. There is no way you can be thirsty?

 No thanks, Elsa.

 Don't mind them.

 It's OK; I'm okay.

 You guys! Take it easy!
At least he had the courage to run.

 Ooh, Ed has a bodyguard.

 There are some things he is good at.

 Like playing in the mud?

 Come right here and say it to my face. I'm so ready for you!

Elsa calm down! Guys, ignore them. Let's go now!

 You know, Ji-hoon, if you hadn't stopped me, I totally would've shown those bullies what's what!

 Well done Elsa. You have learned to think before you react.

 I'm still a work in progress. Thank God you were there.

 Settle down, class. Take out your drawings and start painting your fruit. Don't forget your band practices. There are only THREE weeks left before the competition.

 El, hope your band's ready to lose. Hope you're as good with instruments as you are with paint. It'll be a shame to see you flop at both.

 Guess you'll have to wait and see. We might just surprise you.

 ENOUGH of that!

 Why green paint?
You don't even like green apples.

 At least you can see it is an apple.
I'm giving the apple some extra flair.
And what's that supposed to be?
The world's largest berry?

 See for yourself.

 I have never seen such a fruit.

 What? Can't you see what it is?

 I'm just joking.
A strawberry and it looks delicious.

 BEHOLD, the ULTIMATE strawberry! Yeah, it's yummy! Do you want some?

 Ultimate, huh? It's so 'ultimate', you've got red all over your face.

 Bet my strawberry can take down any bully.

  HAHA!

 AAH! Ouch!

 What happened? Ed, are you okay?

 Oh, not again! Didn't he fall enough today? HAHAHA!

 Ed, what's up? Maybe he thought it was the finish line. HAHAHA!

 That's ENOUGH from you all!
Ed, are you hurt?
Ji-hoon, please take him to the washroom.

 Ji-hoon, leave me alone.

 How did the snake get rid of the paint?

 Huh, what are you saying?

 It shed its skin.  Is that supposed to be a joke?

 It's drier than the desert.

 Exactly! I am terrible at telling jokes.

  HAHA!

 Walk home with us. We'll see you at the gate.

 Okay, at least come to Ji-hoon's house tomorrow and give us some tips.
His mom makes the best South Korean snacks.

 Okay.

 Cheers, we'll see you tomorrow.

 Cheers.

 Hi, welcome to the K-POP Rock Stars!

 Do you know this song?

 I love this song.

 OK, grab that mic and sing with us.

 We have a guitar, but no one to play it.

 I can play guitar. I've been playing since I was four.

 GREAT! Let's do this.

 What key are we playing in?

 'Giraffe.'

 What?

 'G' my friend!    HAHA!

3 WEEKS LATER…

 Let's take a break.
Try some of my mom's bungeoppang.

 No, thank you. I don't eat fish.

 Haha, it's not fish. It's a fish-shaped pastry with Nutella on the inside. Try it. It's delicious.

 Ooh, my favourite. Yummy!
Aunt Ji-min's pastries are YUMMILICIOUS.

HAHA!

 Well done, team. We've been practising every day for three weeks. We are ready!

 I'm a little nervous. Tomorrow is the big day.

 We will SMASH IT! Go, K-POP Rock Stars!

 Leave me! You and Elsa can sing alone.

 Yeah, we can, but we aren't a band without you. You have been blessed with amazing talent, and you have no idea how good you are. I mean, God has given you this talent, Ed!

 I don't know, Ji-hoon. I'm…

 They can call you names, and take away your stuff but don't allow them to take the greatness within you. You will run away with the individual award.

 You are by far the best. This is your game. Those bullies are trying to cover up their insecurities. They are all bark and no bite, all talk and no action. They only have as much power as you give them. Right now Jesus Christ will strengthen you, just step out like David did.

 I have never heard you speak like this, like God, Jesus, and who, … David and stuff. You really want me to go back on stage?

 Hahaha! My life is all about Jesus; we will speak about this later. But right now, yes! Go and show what you are best at. Get your act together. You will prove them wrong!

OK! Let's do this.

WHAT WOULD JESUS DO?

Wow, Ji-hoon, wasn't today just epic?
Ed totally flipped the script on those bullies!

It really was. It reminds me of David and Goliath.
Ed might not have looked like much to those bullies,
just as David didn't look like a war champion to Goliath.

Ah, I love that story! So, Ed's guitar is like David's
slingshot and his voice is like those anointed stones.

Yes, Goliath bullied the Israelite armies, but the
Word of God in David's heart was his weapon.
I thank God that today He gave me the Words to
encourage Ed so that he could step out like David did.

Yes! When Ed appeared on stage,
it was a MIRACLE!

We thank God for everything.

 I also learned to stand up for those who are bullied and for those who are weak.

 Absolutely! The Bible tells us to stand up for what's right and to have courage. God supports us, like He supported David and we should always have our friends' backs. All of us have strengths and weaknesses. Where I am weak, you are strong. Where you are weak, I am strong.

 Yeah! We are one another's strength!
SUPER AWESOME JESUS!

 What is also awesome is that Ed didn't give u

Yes! Never give up!
Never Surrender!
Let's KEEP ROCKING
IT FOR JESUS!

LET'S PRAY

Father, may Your Spirit who dwells in my heart
be the voice of my prayer, in Jesus' name.

Jesus, You love everyone in this world;
both good and bad. Help me to love as You love.

Help me to use my mouth to build people up and not destroy.

Help me to stand for what is right.

In Jesus' name.

Amen.

BIBLE VERSES TO CHECK OUT

Joshua 1:9, 1 Samuel 17:1-51, Proverbs 31:8-9,

Ecclesiastes 4:9-10, 1 Peter 4:8-10, Acts 20:35, John 3:16

INSPIRATIONAL QUOTES

Know that you are unique and that no one else is like you; stop comparing yourself to others.

Psalm 139:13-16, Isaiah 43:1, Jeremiah 1:5, Matthew 10:30

Do you know that your smile or greeting may just be what someone needs to brighten their day?

Proverbs 15:30, 16:24, Luke 10:25-37, Philippians 2:4, Hebrews 13:1-2

A little act of kindness can meet a need and change a life.

Matthew 10:42, Luke 10:25-37, Galatians 6:10, Hebrews 13:16

When you reject a buddy because of his flaws, you also reject his strengths.

Judges 11:1-12, 1 Samuel 16:1-13, Mark 6:3, John 7:5-7

Because you have failed in one area doesn't mean you're a failure.

Genesis 39-41, Proverbs 16:3, Isaiah 43:18-19, Jeremiah 29:11, Philippians 4:13

LET'S CHAT

You heard what Ji-hoon said to Ed. How would you have encouraged Ed?
_____
_____
_____

What's one lesson you learned from how Ji-hoon stood up to the bullies?
_____
_____
_____

How did Ji-hoon and Elsa prove to be Bully-Proof Friends?
_____
_____
_____

Ask yourself. How can I be a Bully-Proof Friend?
_____
_____
_____

What did you enjoy about this story? How does this story inspire you?
_____
_____
_____

What gave David, a shepherd boy, the courage to face Goliath?
_____
_____
_____

OTHER BOOKS IN
THE WHAT WOULD JESUS DO SERIES

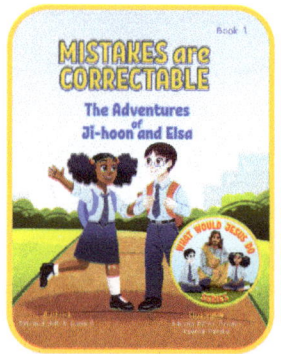
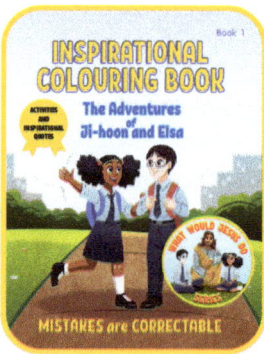

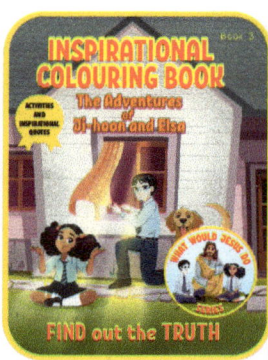

OTHER BOOKS BY THE AUTHORS

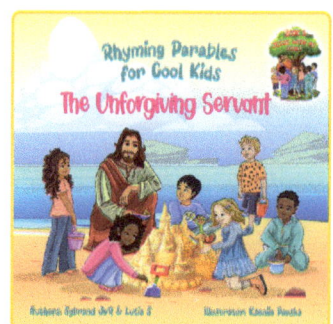
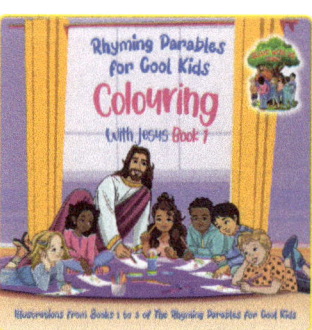